AI AND THE STAKEHOLDER REVOLUTION

Creating and Destroying Value in a Rapidly Changing World

CONSULTORIA IA

Copyright © 2024 CONSULTORIA IA

All rights reserved

The characters and events portrayed in this book are fictitious. Any similarity to real persons, living or dead, is coincidental and not intended by the author.

No part of this book may be reproduced, or stored in a retrieval system, or transmitted in any form or by any means, electronic, mechanical, photocopying, recording, or otherwise, without express written permission of the publisher.

Cover design by: Art Painter
Library of Congress Control Number: 2018675309
Printed in the United States of America

TO OUR FAMILY

CONTENTS

Title Page
Copyright
Dedication
Brief Overview
Target Audience
Why Read This Book?
Preface
Chapter 1: The Rise of AI in the Stakeholder Era
Chapter 2: Redefining Value: Opportunities and Ethical Dilemmas
Chapter 3: The New Power Dynamics: AI, Governance, and Corporate Responsibility
Chapter 4: Balancing Innovation and Inclusion
Chapter 5: Future-Proofing Organizations in a Rapidly Changing World
Appendices

BRIEF OVERVIEW

AI and the Stakeholder Revolution: Creating and Destroying Value in a Rapidly Changing World explores the profound impact of artificial intelligence on the evolving dynamics of stakeholder capitalism. As businesses face increasing pressure to balance profit with purpose, this book examines how AI is reshaping industries, redefining stakeholder relationships, and influencing the pursuit of sustainable growth.

The book provides insights into AI's dual role: as a tool for value creation through innovation, efficiency, and personalization, and as a disruptor that can challenge traditional business models, ethical frameworks, and workforce dynamics. It highlights case studies of companies navigating these challenges, offering practical strategies for leveraging AI responsibly while fostering trust among stakeholders.

With a focus on ethical AI practices, corporate accountability, and the role of leadership in an AI-driven era, this book is a timely guide for executives, policymakers, and anyone interested in the intersection of technology, business, and society.

TARGET AUDIENCE

The target audience for **AI and the Stakeholder Revolution: Creating and Destroying Value in a Rapidly Changing World** includes:

1. **Business Leaders and Executives**
   - CEOs, managers, and decision-makers looking to understand the impact of AI on stakeholder relationships and value creation in their industries.
2. **Policymakers and Regulators**
   - Professionals crafting policies for ethical AI use, corporate accountability, and sustainable economic development.
3. **Entrepreneurs and Innovators**
   - Startups and innovators aiming to harness AI for growth while navigating stakeholder demands and ethical considerations.
4. **Academics and Researchers**
   - Scholars in business, economics, and technology seeking to explore the intersection of AI and stakeholder capitalism.
5. **Investors and Financial Analysts**
   - Individuals analyzing AI's influence on market trends, company valuation, and long-term sustainability.
6. **Students and Educators**
   - Learners in business, technology, and public policy eager to understand how AI is reshaping the global economy and organizational dynamics.
7. **General Readers with Interest in AI and Society**
   - Anyone curious about the ethical, social, and economic implications of AI in the modern world.

WHY READ THIS BOOK?

1. **Understand AI's Transformative Impact**
   - Discover how AI is reshaping industries, redefining business models, and influencing corporate strategies in the context of stakeholder capitalism.
2. **Navigate Ethical and Social Challenges**
   - Gain insights into the ethical dilemmas and societal impacts of AI, with practical guidance on responsible and sustainable AI integration.
3. **Learn from Real-World Case Studies**
   - Explore compelling examples of companies that have successfully leveraged AI for stakeholder value—and those that faced setbacks—providing actionable lessons.
4. **Prepare for the Future of Work and Leadership**
   - Understand the evolving role of leaders and the workforce in an AI-driven world, with strategies to foster innovation while maintaining trust and accountability.
5. **Bridge Profit and Purpose**
   - Discover how to balance profitability with the demands of diverse stakeholders, from employees and customers to communities and investors.
6. **Stay Competitive in a Rapidly Changing World**
   - Equip yourself with knowledge and strategies to remain relevant and competitive as AI continues to accelerate change across industries.

Whether you're a business leader, policymaker, entrepreneur, or simply curious about the future of AI and society, this book offers critical insights to thrive in the age of disruption.

PREFACE

We are living in a time of unprecedented change. The rise of artificial intelligence (AI) is not merely an evolution of technology—it's a revolution reshaping the very fabric of business, society, and human interaction. From transforming industries to redefining relationships between corporations and their stakeholders, AI stands at the center of a global paradigm shift.

This book, **AI and the Stakeholder Revolution**, was born out of a simple yet pressing question: *How can we harness the transformative power of AI to create value for all stakeholders in a sustainable and equitable way?*

Over the past decade, businesses have faced increasing pressure to go beyond profits and address the needs of their employees, customers, communities, and the environment. Simultaneously, the rapid pace of AI development has introduced both immense opportunities and significant challenges. At the intersection of these forces lies a critical moment of choice—one that will determine whether AI serves as a tool for shared prosperity or a driver of deeper inequalities and ethical dilemmas.

In this book, I aim to explore this intersection, offering a balanced perspective on how organizations can navigate this complexity. Through case studies, data-driven insights, and practical frameworks, I delve into how AI can be used to create value responsibly while fostering trust and long-term success.

I also address the darker side of this revolution: the ways AI can destroy value—undermining trust, widening inequalities, and exacerbating risks. Recognizing these potential pitfalls is essential to building a future where AI benefits all stakeholders.

Ultimately, this book is an invitation—to business leaders, policymakers, innovators, and citizens alike—to rethink how we define success in an AI-driven world. Together, we have the power to shape this revolution into one that creates sustainable value for everyone.

Welcome to the stakeholder revolution. Let's ensure that AI is a force for good.

Consultoria IA
Seville, Spain
2024

CHAPTER 1: THE RISE OF AI IN THE STAKEHOLDER ERA

The 21st century marks the dawn of a new era: one where businesses no longer exist solely to maximize shareholder returns but to serve a broader ecosystem of stakeholders. Customers, employees, suppliers, communities, and the planet itself now demand a voice in corporate boardrooms. This shift toward stakeholder capitalism is redefining the purpose of enterprise, and at the heart of this transformation lies the unprecedented rise of artificial intelligence (AI). No longer confined to the pages of science fiction, AI has rapidly evolved into a disruptive force capable of creating, reshaping, and at times, obliterating value across industries. But how did we get here, and why is AI uniquely positioned to lead this revolution?

The Convergence of Technology and Responsibility

AI's emergence as a transformative tool coincides with a critical inflection point in global business. For decades, corporations adhered to the doctrine of shareholder primacy, popularized by economist Milton Friedman in the 1970s. Success was measured in quarterly earnings, cost-cutting efficiencies, and stock price performance. However, mounting crises—ranging from environmental degradation and widening inequality to geopolitical instability and eroding trust in institutions—have challenged this narrow definition of value creation. Stakeholders today demand not just profitability but purpose, sustainability, and inclusivity.

Enter AI, a technology that thrives on data—the digital DNA of our interconnected world. Its ability to process, analyze, and predict at scale provides an unparalleled advantage for businesses looking to navigate the complexities of stakeholder demands. Whether it's optimizing supply chains to reduce carbon footprints, predicting customer needs to enhance satisfaction, or enabling more equitable hiring practices, AI has become the linchpin of a stakeholder-centric approach to business.

But AI is not a silver bullet. Its duality as a creator and destroyer of value raises profound questions. For every efficiency gained through automation, jobs may be displaced. For every personalized customer experience, there may be an erosion of privacy. The rise of AI in the stakeholder era requires a delicate balancing act: leveraging its potential for good while mitigating its inherent risks.

AI as the Catalyst for Stakeholder Collaboration

Perhaps AI's most transformative quality lies in its ability to break down silos and foster collaboration. Traditional business models often pit stakeholders against one another—workers versus employers, communities versus corporations, and environmentalists versus industrialists. AI, however, has the potential to align these seemingly conflicting interests through data-driven insights and transparency.

Take, for instance, the role of AI in sustainable business practices. Advanced algorithms can analyze entire supply chains to identify inefficiencies and environmental hotspots, enabling companies to reduce waste and emissions while saving costs. This not only satisfies shareholders seeking efficiency but also aligns with the values of environmentally conscious consumers and regulators. Similarly, AI-driven workforce analytics can create win-win scenarios by identifying skills gaps and enabling upskilling programs that benefit both employees and employers.

AI also empowers stakeholders to hold corporations accountable. Tools that leverage natural language processing can analyze public sentiment, track corporate promises, and flag inconsistencies in real-time. This democratization of information ensures that businesses can no longer pay lip service to stakeholder concerns—they must deliver measurable outcomes.

The Global Context: Why Timing Matters

The rise of AI in the stakeholder era is not occurring in a vacuum. It is deeply intertwined with global megatrends such as digital transformation, demographic shifts, and the growing urgency of climate change. The COVID-19 pandemic, in particular, served as a wake-up call for businesses to rethink their priorities. Companies that adapted swiftly to remote work, digital operations, and new customer behaviors not only survived but thrived. Many of these adaptations were powered by AI, from chatbots handling customer inquiries to algorithms optimizing vaccine distribution.

This context underscores why timing is critical. The convergence of these trends creates a once-in-a-generation opportunity to embed stakeholder values into the DNA of business, with AI as the enabler. However, this window is not infinite. As AI adoption accelerates, so do its risks—bias in algorithms, cybersecurity threats, and the potential monopolization of AI capabilities by a few dominant players. The choices we make today will determine whether AI serves as a tool for empowerment or a weapon for exploitation.

Ethical Imperatives in the Age of AI

At the heart of AI's role in the stakeholder era is the question of ethics. How can companies ensure that AI aligns with the values and expectations of all stakeholders? This challenge requires a proactive approach, starting with transparency. Businesses must demystify AI by explaining how algorithms work, what data they use, and what outcomes they generate. Stakeholders need to trust that AI is being deployed responsibly, without hidden agendas or unintended consequences.

Fairness is another critical consideration. From hiring practices to credit scoring, AI systems must be free from bias that could perpetuate inequality. This requires continuous monitoring, diverse datasets, and human oversight to ensure that AI decisions are equitable. Companies that neglect these safeguards risk reputational damage, regulatory penalties, and, most importantly, a breach of stakeholder trust.

Finally, the ethical use of AI must address the broader implications of automation. While AI can drive efficiency and innovation, it can also displace workers and disrupt industries. Businesses have a responsibility to anticipate these impacts and invest in reskilling programs, social safety nets, and alternative career pathways. AI should not be viewed as a zero-sum game but as a means to elevate the collective potential of society.

Looking Ahead: The AI-Driven Stakeholder Revolution

As we stand at the crossroads of technological innovation and societal transformation, it is clear that AI's role in the stakeholder era is just beginning. The decisions made by today's leaders will shape the trajectory of industries, economies, and communities for decades to come.

For businesses, the imperative is clear: embrace AI not as a standalone tool but as an integrated framework for stakeholder engagement. This means going beyond short-term profits to create long-term value that benefits all. For policymakers, the challenge is to establish guardrails that encourage innovation while protecting against misuse. And for individuals, the responsibility lies in staying informed, vocal, and active in shaping the ethical boundaries of AI.

The rise of AI in the stakeholder era is not just a story of technological progress; it is a call to action for humanity. By aligning AI's capabilities with stakeholder values, we have the opportunity to create a future that is not only more efficient but also more equitable, sustainable, and inclusive. The question is not whether AI will define this new era—it already has. The question is: how will we harness its power to define it on our terms?

From Shareholder Primacy to Stakeholder Inclusivity: AI as a Transformative Force

The traditional doctrine of shareholder primacy—where maximizing profits and shareholder returns was the sole purpose of business—has increasingly fallen out of favor. In its place, a more holistic approach has emerged: stakeholder inclusivity. This paradigm recognizes that businesses have responsibilities beyond profits, encompassing their employees, customers, communities, suppliers, and the environment. At the forefront of this transformation is artificial intelligence (AI), a technology that is not only driving efficiencies but also reshaping how organizations interact with and create value for their stakeholders.

AI's potential to enable transparency, sustainability, and accountability makes it uniquely suited to champion the shift toward stakeholder inclusivity. However, its role is complex and multifaceted, often raising new challenges as it solves others. This chapter delves into AI's transformative role, citing emblematic cases, data, and insights to highlight its profound impact.

The End of Shareholder Primacy: A Tectonic Shift

For decades, the Friedman doctrine of shareholder primacy reigned supreme. Companies focused on short-term profits, sometimes at the expense of long-term stability and societal well-being. However, this model began to crack under the weight of global crises, such as climate change, economic inequality, and growing demands for corporate accountability.

In 2019, the Business Roundtable, a group of nearly 200 CEOs from major U.S. companies, made headlines by redefining the purpose of a corporation. They declared a commitment to deliver value to all stakeholders, not just shareholders. This marked a seismic shift in corporate philosophy, signaling that businesses must serve a broader purpose.

AI, with its ability to analyze vast amounts of data and generate actionable insights, is playing a pivotal role in turning these ideals into actionable strategies. For instance, AI-driven platforms enable real-time monitoring of sustainability efforts, while machine learning algorithms predict stakeholder needs with unprecedented accuracy.

AI's Role in Stakeholder Inclusivity

1. Sustainability and the Environment

AI has become an indispensable tool in the fight against climate change, helping organizations reduce their environmental impact while meeting stakeholder demands for sustainable practices.

- **Case Study: Google's Carbon-Reduction Efforts**
  Google has utilized AI to optimize its data centers, which account for significant energy consumption. By employing DeepMind's AI algorithms, the company reduced energy use for cooling by 40%, achieving both cost savings and environmental benefits.

- **Statistical Impact**
  A report by PwC estimates that AI applications in agriculture, energy, and transportation could reduce global greenhouse gas emissions by up to 4% by 2030—equivalent to removing 2.4 billion tons of CO_2 annually.

AI's predictive capabilities also enable businesses to manage resources more effectively. For example, supply chain platforms use AI to forecast demand and minimize waste, aligning profitability with sustainability goals.

2. Employee Empowerment and Workforce Transformation

AI is revolutionizing workforce management, creating opportunities to enhance employee satisfaction and productivity while addressing concerns about automation and job displacement.

- **Case Study: Unilever and AI-Driven Recruitment**
  Unilever transformed its hiring process by leveraging AI to screen candidates, analyze facial expressions, and predict job performance. This not only reduced hiring bias but also shortened the recruitment cycle by 75%.

- **Balancing Risks**
  While AI can enhance workforce efficiency, it also raises concerns about job displacement. According to a McKinsey report, up to 25% of jobs in the U.S. may be automated by 2030. However, the same report highlights that AI could create new roles, particularly in fields like data science, AI ethics, and system integration.

To address these challenges, companies must invest in reskilling and upskilling programs. IBM, for instance, has pledged to train 30 million people in AI-related skills by 2030, ensuring that workers remain relevant in an AI-driven economy.

3. Customer-Centric Innovation

AI is redefining customer engagement by personalizing experiences and anticipating needs. This shift aligns businesses with their stakeholders' expectations for seamless, value-driven interactions.

- **Case Study: Amazon's AI-Powered Recommendations**
  Amazon uses AI to analyze purchasing behaviors and provide personalized product recommendations, contributing to 35% of the company's total sales. This not only drives revenue but also enhances customer satisfaction.

- **Consumer Expectations**
  A Salesforce study revealed that 76% of customers expect companies to understand their needs and expectations. AI enables businesses to meet these demands by analyzing vast amounts of customer data, ensuring tailored solutions that foster loyalty.

4. Community and Social Responsibility

AI's ability to analyze social trends and public sentiment allows companies to align their initiatives with community needs, fostering trust and goodwill.

- **Case Study: Microsoft's AI for Good Initiative**
  Microsoft has committed $165 million to its AI for Good program, which leverages AI to address societal challenges, from disaster response to healthcare accessibility. One example is the "AI for Earth" initiative, which supports projects aimed at improving water quality and agriculture through AI.

- **Building Accountability**
  Natural language processing tools allow organizations to monitor public sentiment, identify emerging issues, and adjust their strategies accordingly. This ensures that community concerns are not just heard but acted upon.

Challenges and Ethical Considerations

While AI holds immense potential, its deployment must be guided by ethical considerations to ensure stakeholder trust.

- **Algorithmic Bias**
  AI systems trained on biased datasets can perpetuate inequality. For example, a study by MIT found that facial recognition software from leading vendors was 34% less accurate for darker-skinned women compared to lighter-skinned men.

- **Data Privacy**
  Stakeholders demand transparency about how their data is used. Companies like Apple have responded by introducing privacy-centric features, such as differential privacy and on-device processing, to safeguard user information.

- **Job Displacement**
  Automation, while driving efficiency, poses a risk to workers. Stakeholder-focused companies must proactively address this by providing safety nets and alternative career pathways.

Ethical AI frameworks, such as those proposed by the OECD and the European Union, offer guidelines for responsible AI adoption. However, these frameworks must be universally adopted to create a level playing field.

The Future of AI and Stakeholder Inclusivity

1. Predictive Analytics for Anticipating Stakeholder Needs

AI's ability to predict trends and behaviors will become increasingly critical. For example, predictive models can help companies anticipate regulatory changes or shifts in consumer preferences, ensuring that they remain ahead of stakeholder expectations.

2. Decentralization and Democratization of AI

To prevent monopolization, companies must focus on democratizing AI access. OpenAI's GPT models, for instance, provide businesses of all sizes with access to powerful AI tools, fostering inclusivity and innovation.

3. AI-Driven Metrics for Stakeholder Value

Traditional financial metrics are no longer sufficient to measure success. AI can analyze non-financial indicators, such as employee engagement, community impact, and environmental sustainability, offering a holistic view of stakeholder value creation.

4. Collaborative Ecosystems

AI will enable cross-sector collaborations, uniting businesses, governments, and non-profits to tackle global challenges. For example, the World Economic Forum's partnership with AI-driven platforms aims to address climate change by pooling resources and expertise.

The shift from shareholder primacy to stakeholder inclusivity marks a profound evolution in the purpose of business. At the heart of this transformation lies AI, a technology capable of balancing profitability with societal responsibility. However, this journey is not without its challenges. The ethical deployment of AI, coupled with a commitment to transparency, fairness, and inclusivity, will determine its role as a force for good.

As businesses navigate this transition, they must embrace AI not as a mere tool but as a catalyst for creating shared value. The path forward is clear: by aligning AI with stakeholder values, we can build a future that is not only prosperous but also equitable, sustainable, and inclusive—a future where technology serves humanity, not the other way around.

CHAPTER 2: REDEFINING VALUE: OPPORTUNITIES AND ETHICAL DILEMMAS

In the dawn of the stakeholder revolution, the notion of value is undergoing a profound transformation. Traditionally, value creation was measured narrowly—profits, shareholder returns, and quarterly earnings were king. However, artificial intelligence (AI) has accelerated the evolution of this paradigm. Today, businesses and societies are grappling with a broader, more inclusive definition of value, one that transcends financial metrics to encompass environmental impact, social equity, and ethical considerations. This shift has opened extraordinary opportunities for innovation and growth, yet it has also unleashed a Pandora's box of ethical dilemmas that cannot be ignored.

The New Value Proposition: Beyond Profit Margins

AI is enabling businesses to deliver value in unprecedented ways. Companies are leveraging AI-powered tools to enhance customer experiences, streamline operations, and predict consumer needs with remarkable precision. Retailers like Amazon use machine learning algorithms to recommend products, while healthcare providers employ AI to diagnose diseases faster and with greater accuracy. These innovations have unlocked massive efficiencies and created a wave of personalized services that were unimaginable just a decade ago.

Yet the rise of AI has forced businesses to reconsider *who* their stakeholders are. Employees, customers, suppliers, communities, and even the planet itself are demanding a seat at the table. A business's ability to cater to this diverse array of interests has become a competitive advantage in the digital age. For example, Patagonia's commitment to environmental sustainability, supported by AI-driven supply chain optimization, has won over eco-conscious consumers and reinforced its brand loyalty. Similarly, Microsoft's AI for Earth initiative aligns technological innovation with environmental stewardship, creating value for both the company and the planet.

But this broader value proposition comes with a caveat. As companies embrace AI to serve a wider array of stakeholders, the complexity of their ethical responsibilities increases. The challenge lies not in creating value but in ensuring that this value is distributed equitably and aligns with the principles of fairness and sustainability.

ETHICAL AI: A DOUBLE-EDGED SWORD

The opportunities presented by AI are immense, but they come with ethical pitfalls that, if left unchecked, could lead to reputational damage, regulatory backlash, and societal harm. One of the most pressing dilemmas is algorithmic bias. AI systems are only as unbiased as the data they are trained on, and when historical data reflects systemic inequalities, AI has the potential to perpetuate or even exacerbate these disparities. For instance, hiring algorithms designed to screen job applicants have, in some cases, systematically favored male candidates over equally qualified females, simply because the training data reflected a male-dominated workforce.

Similarly, the use of AI in law enforcement has raised alarms. Predictive policing algorithms, designed to allocate resources more efficiently, have been criticized for disproportionately targeting minority communities. These examples highlight a fundamental question: Who decides what is fair?

Businesses must approach AI development with an ethical framework that prioritizes transparency, accountability, and inclusivity. Implementing bias audits, diversifying datasets, and involving ethicists in AI design are essential steps to ensure these systems serve humanity equitably. Leaders must also embrace a culture of responsibility, recognizing that short-term gains achieved through ethically dubious practices could lead to long-term consequences that erode trust and value.

Transparency vs. Privacy: The Great Trade-Off

In the era of big data, transparency has become a buzzword. Consumers increasingly demand to know how their data is collected, stored, and used, while regulators worldwide are implementing stricter data privacy laws such as GDPR in Europe and CCPA in California. AI thrives on data, but its hunger for information creates a tension between transparency and privacy.

Consider the healthcare industry, where AI-driven systems analyze patient data to predict illnesses and recommend treatments. These technologies have the potential to save lives, but they require access to sensitive personal information. Striking the right balance between leveraging data for societal benefit and safeguarding individual privacy is a dilemma that every organization must grapple with.

Tech giants like Apple have taken a proactive stance by embedding privacy-first principles into their AI systems. For example, Apple's on-device processing ensures that sensitive user data never leaves the user's device, reducing the risk of breaches. This approach demonstrates that privacy and innovation are not mutually exclusive. However, not all companies prioritize privacy, and lapses can lead to devastating consequences, as seen in high-profile cases like the Cambridge Analytica scandal.

THE ENVIRONMENTAL COST OF AI

Another often-overlooked aspect of AI's value proposition is its environmental impact. Training large AI models requires enormous computational power, which in turn consumes significant energy. According to recent studies, training a single AI model can emit as much carbon dioxide as five cars over their lifetime.

This environmental cost clashes with the growing demand for sustainability. Stakeholders increasingly expect businesses to demonstrate environmental responsibility, and AI's carbon footprint has the potential to become a reputational risk. Companies like Google and OpenAI have started investing in renewable energy and developing energy-efficient AI models, setting a precedent for sustainable innovation.

Yet the question remains: Is it enough? As AI continues to scale, businesses must explore more radical solutions, such as carbon offsets, partnerships with green energy providers, and investments in quantum computing, which promises to be far more energy-efficient than traditional AI systems.

Redefining Success in the Stakeholder Era

In this new age of stakeholder capitalism, success can no longer be measured solely by financial performance. Instead, it requires a holistic approach that integrates economic, social, and environmental metrics. AI plays a pivotal role in enabling this transformation. Tools like natural language processing can analyze consumer sentiment to gauge brand reputation, while machine learning models assess the impact of corporate initiatives on community well-being.

However, redefining success also demands cultural change. Leaders must embrace a mindset that values long-term resilience over short-term gains. Patagonia's decision to prioritize environmental responsibility over profit margins illustrates how businesses can align their goals with stakeholder interests without sacrificing growth.

The integration of AI into this framework offers a unique advantage. By leveraging AI to gather insights and predict trends, organizations can anticipate stakeholder needs and proactively adapt their strategies. Companies that fail to evolve risk being left behind, as consumers, employees, and investors increasingly favor businesses that demonstrate a commitment to broader societal values.

NAVIGATING THE ETHICAL LANDSCAPE

As the lines between technology and humanity blur, navigating the ethical landscape of AI becomes a critical imperative. Businesses must ask themselves: What kind of world are we building with AI? This question requires leaders to adopt a moral compass that goes beyond compliance and embraces the principles of justice, equity, and sustainability.

Developing AI systems with ethical considerations at the forefront is not just a moral obligation but a business necessity. Trust, once lost, is nearly impossible to regain, and organizations that fail to uphold ethical standards risk alienating their stakeholders. The path forward lies in collaboration. Governments, businesses, and civil society must work together to establish ethical guidelines that ensure AI serves humanity as a force for good.

The Call to Action

The opportunities offered by AI are unparalleled, but they come with a responsibility to create value that benefits all stakeholders. This chapter has explored the dual-edged nature of AI—a technology that can either elevate humanity or exacerbate its divides. The choice lies in the hands of businesses, governments, and individuals.

To succeed in the age of the stakeholder revolution, organizations must redefine value in ways that embrace innovation, prioritize ethics, and ensure sustainability. It is a daunting challenge, but it is also a defining opportunity. As stewards of this transformative technology, we hold the power to shape a future that reflects the best of human potential.

The Dual Nature of AI: Creating and Destroying Value Across Industries

Artificial Intelligence (AI) has transformed industries at an unprecedented pace, reshaping markets, revolutionizing business models, and generating extraordinary value. However, it also introduces risks that could undermine its promise. From healthcare to finance, AI creates opportunities for efficiency, innovation, and growth, but it can also disrupt labor markets, deepen societal inequities, and perpetuate systemic biases. The pressing question is: *how do we harness AI's potential while addressing its ethical and societal challenges?*

Let's dive into this question through three key lenses: **How does AI generate economic value? Where does it destroy value? What are the ethical and societal implications of its widespread adoption?**

Question 1: How Does AI Create Economic Value Across Industries?

AI creates value by automating processes, enhancing decision-making, and opening new revenue streams. Its capabilities are revolutionizing sectors like healthcare, manufacturing, and retail.

Healthcare: Saving Lives and Costs

AI's impact on healthcare is profound. Machine learning algorithms can analyze medical data to identify diseases earlier and with greater accuracy than human practitioners. For example, AI-driven diagnostic tools have achieved a 94.5% accuracy rate in detecting breast cancer from mammograms, compared to an average accuracy rate of 88% for radiologists.

In monetary terms, McKinsey estimates that AI could generate up to **$360 billion annually in global healthcare savings** by improving diagnosis, optimizing treatment plans, and reducing administrative inefficiencies. Startups like Tempus and DeepMind are developing AI solutions to streamline drug discovery, cutting development costs by 30-50%.

Manufacturing: Unlocking Efficiency

In manufacturing, AI-driven robotics and predictive analytics have revolutionized production lines. AI-enabled predictive maintenance systems, for instance, can identify machine faults before they occur, reducing downtime by up to 50% and increasing operational efficiency by 20-30%. According to PwC, AI applications in manufacturing could add **$1.4 trillion to the global economy by 2030**, primarily by increasing productivity and reducing waste.

Retail: Personalization at Scale

Retailers are using AI to create hyper-personalized shopping experiences. Amazon's recommendation engine, powered by machine learning, generates 35% of the company's revenue. Similarly, AI chatbots are transforming customer service, handling 70-80% of routine inquiries without human intervention, reducing labor costs and improving response times.

Across industries, the scalability of AI allows businesses to enhance their value propositions, serve customers more effectively, and generate significant economic returns. However, these benefits come with challenges, including the displacement of human labor and the potential for monopolistic practices.

Question 2: Where Does AI Destroy Value?

Despite its promise, AI has a destructive side. It threatens job security, exacerbates inequalities, and introduces risks that undermine trust in technology and institutions.

Labor Displacement: Automation's Double-Edged Sword

AI-driven automation is poised to displace millions of jobs. According to a report by the World Economic Forum, **85 million jobs could be displaced by 2025**, primarily in roles involving repetitive tasks such as data entry, assembly line work, and retail operations.

Take the case of autonomous vehicles. The trucking industry employs over 3.5 million drivers in the U.S. alone. With companies like Tesla and Waymo advancing self-driving technology, these jobs are at risk of obsolescence, creating a ripple effect in industries like logistics, fueling stations, and roadside services.

While AI creates new roles—such as AI ethicists and machine learning engineers—it often requires highly specialized skills. This disparity contributes to a growing divide between high- and low-skilled workers. Without targeted reskilling programs, the displacement caused by AI could exacerbate economic inequalities, potentially costing the global economy **$8.5 trillion in lost productivity by 2030**, as estimated by the International Labour Organization.

Ethical Breaches: Trust Erosion

AI's potential to destroy value extends beyond economics to trust. High-profile scandals, such as Facebook-Cambridge Analytica, where AI algorithms were used to manipulate voter behavior, have raised concerns about the misuse of AI in society.

The financial sector, too, is grappling with trust issues. AI trading algorithms have caused "flash crashes" in stock markets, wiping out billions of dollars in market value within minutes. These incidents highlight the risks of delegating high-stakes decisions to opaque AI systems, eroding trust in markets and institutions.

Environmental Costs: AI's Carbon Footprint

Training large AI models is resource-intensive. For instance, training GPT-3 required 1287 MWh of electricity and emitted **550 metric tons of CO_2**, equivalent to the annual emissions of 120 cars. As businesses scale their AI operations, the environmental toll threatens to undermine sustainability goals, particularly in energy-intensive industries like cloud computing and blockchain.

Question 3: What Are the Ethical and Societal Impacts of AI Adoption?

The societal impacts of AI adoption are vast, ranging from privacy concerns to algorithmic bias. The ethical dilemmas surrounding AI reflect deeper questions about power, fairness, and responsibility.

Privacy: The Cost of Big Data

AI thrives on data, but its hunger for information raises significant privacy concerns. In China, AI-powered surveillance systems with facial recognition monitor public spaces, sparking debates about the trade-off between safety and privacy. In democracies, scandals such as Clearview AI's unauthorized scraping of billions of online photos for law enforcement use illustrate how AI can blur the lines between innovation and intrusion.

Public awareness is growing: A 2023 Pew Research survey found that **72% of Americans** are concerned about how companies use their personal data. This mistrust can lead to consumer backlash, regulatory fines, and reputational damage, as evidenced by the $5 billion penalty levied against Facebook for data privacy violations in 2019.

Algorithmic Bias: Deepening Inequality

AI's reliance on historical data can perpetuate societal biases. For instance, AI recruitment tools trained on predominantly male data have exhibited gender discrimination, rejecting qualified female candidates. Similarly, facial recognition software has been found to have error rates of up to 35% for darker-skinned individuals compared to less than 1% for lighter-skinned ones.

These biases not only harm marginalized groups but also expose businesses to legal and reputational risks. A study by IBM estimated that biased AI could cost global organizations **$12 billion annually** due to lawsuits, brand erosion, and regulatory penalties.

Autonomous Weapons: The Dark Side of AI

Perhaps the gravest ethical concern is the militarization of AI. Autonomous weapons, often dubbed "killer robots," can make life-and-death decisions without human intervention. While proponents argue that AI can reduce human casualties in warfare, critics warn of unintended escalation and the erosion of accountability in conflict zones.

A report by the United Nations has called for a global ban on lethal autonomous weapons, citing the risk of misuse by rogue states and non-state actors. The ethical implications of AI in warfare underscore the urgent need for international agreements to regulate its deployment.

A Path Forward: Mitigating Risks and Maximizing Value

To ensure AI creates more value than it destroys, stakeholders must adopt proactive strategies.

Education and Reskilling

Governments and businesses must invest in reskilling programs to prepare workers for AI-driven economies. Organizations like Amazon have pledged **$700 million** to upskill 100,000 employees by 2025, demonstrating how proactive measures can mitigate labor displacement.

Ethical AI Design

Companies must embed ethical principles into AI development. Microsoft has created an "AI Ethics and Effects in Engineering and Research" (AETHER) committee to oversee its AI projects, ensuring transparency and accountability. Similar initiatives should become industry standards to build public trust.

Environmental Sustainability

AI innovation must align with sustainability goals. Investing in energy-efficient models and renewable energy can reduce AI's carbon footprint. Google has achieved carbon neutrality since 2007, setting an example for balancing technological progress with environmental stewardship.

The Stakes of the AI Revolution

AI has the potential to transform industries and societies for the better, but its adoption must be guided by ethical and societal considerations. Its ability to create value is matched by its capacity to destroy it, making thoughtful regulation, responsible innovation, and collective action essential.

As we navigate this era of rapid change, the question is not whether AI will redefine value, but how we will ensure that this value aligns with humanity's best interests. The choices made today will shape the opportunities and risks of tomorrow—a sobering reminder that the future of AI is not just technological, but profoundly human.

AI's Impact Across Industries: Summary Table

Aspect	Sector/Area	Positive Impact (Value Creation)	Negative Impact (Value Destruction)	Key Figures
Healthcare	Diagnosis & Treatment	Earlier, accurate diagnostics; cost reduction in treatments.	Privacy concerns; dependency on AI over human judgment.	$360 billion annual savings potential (McKinsey).
Manufacturing	Production Efficiency	Predictive maintenance; reduced downtime; increased productivity.	Job displacement in routine manufacturing tasks.	$1.4 trillion added to the global economy by 2030 (PwC).
Retail	Personalization	Enhanced customer experience; revenue growth from AI tools.	Potential misuse of data for manipulative targeting.	35% of Amazon's revenue generated by AI recommendation engines.
Labor Markets	Automation	New roles in AI development; reduced costs for repetitive tasks.	85 million jobs displaced by 2025 (World Economic Forum).	Potential $8.5 trillion loss in global productivity by 2030 (ILO).
Financial Sector	Algorithmic Trading	Faster, data-driven trading decisions; optimized investment returns.	Market instability; flash crashes; erosion of trust.	Billions wiped out in flash crashes due to AI-driven market anomalies.
Environmental Impact	Carbon Emissions	AI-driven energy optimizations in some sectors.	High carbon footprint of AI model training.	550 metric tons of CO_2 for training GPT-3 (equivalent to emissions of 120 cars).
Ethics & Privacy	Data Utilization	Innovations in big data and analytics; societal safety enhancements.	Privacy violations; misuse of personal data.	72% of Americans concerned about corporate data use (Pew Research).
Algorithmic Bias	Recruitment, Policing	Efficiencies in pattern recognition and decision-making.	Perpetuation of systemic biases and inequality.	Biased AI costs $12 billion annually due to lawsuits and brand erosion (IBM).
Autonomous Weapons	Military Applications	Reduced human casualties; precision in warfare.	Lack of accountability; risk of unintended escalation.	UN reports warn against autonomous weapons misuse by rogue entities.

CHAPTER 3: THE NEW POWER DYNAMICS: AI, GOVERNANCE, AND CORPORATE RESPONSIBILITY

In the 21st century, the rise of artificial intelligence (AI) has not only transformed industries but has also redefined the very nature of power. For corporations, governments, and society at large, this technological revolution represents a seismic shift in the way decisions are made, resources are allocated, and responsibilities are shared. AI's influence is no longer confined to optimizing supply chains or personalizing marketing campaigns—it is a force reshaping the social contract between businesses and their stakeholders. Governance, accountability, and the expectations of corporate responsibility are evolving in ways that demand leaders not only adopt AI but also wield it with care, foresight, and a deep commitment to ethical principles.

The integration of AI into governance structures is altering the power dynamics within organizations. Decision-making, once a largely human endeavor, is now increasingly informed—or outright determined—by algorithms. These algorithms can process vast amounts of data at speeds incomprehensible to human minds, enabling organizations to act with unprecedented efficiency. However, the delegation of decisions to AI raises profound questions: Who is accountable when AI makes mistakes? Can stakeholders trust a machine to act in their best interests? And how do organizations ensure that their AI systems are transparent and free from bias?

In practice, governance structures must evolve to address these questions head-on. Traditional corporate boards and executive teams, accustomed to managing risks associated with human decisions, now face the challenge of overseeing complex AI systems. This requires a new kind of leadership—one that combines technical acumen with ethical clarity. Boards must include members who understand AI's capabilities and limitations, ensuring that they can critically evaluate its applications and implications. Furthermore, companies must implement frameworks to audit AI systems regularly, addressing potential biases, inaccuracies, and unintended consequences before they escalate into reputational crises or regulatory penalties.

Beyond internal governance, the role of AI in shaping corporate responsibility is becoming increasingly significant. Stakeholders—including customers, employees, investors, and communities—now expect organizations to use AI not only to generate profits but also to create positive social and environmental impact. The era of shareholder primacy is giving way to the stakeholder revolution, a movement that demands businesses balance the interests of all parties affected by their actions. In this context, AI can be both an enabler and a disruptor of corporate responsibility.

For example, AI-driven analytics can help companies identify and address inefficiencies in their environmental practices, reducing waste and lowering carbon footprints. Predictive models can anticipate social risks in supply chains, such as labor violations or community displacement, allowing companies to take proactive measures. Yet, these same technologies can also amplify harm if misused. Algorithms designed to optimize profitability might inadvertently perpetuate discriminatory practices, exploit vulnerable workers, or prioritize short-term gains over long-term sustainability. The dual potential of AI—to create and destroy value—places a heavy burden on corporate leaders to act with wisdom and accountability.

One of the most visible arenas where AI intersects with corporate responsibility is the labor market. Automation, driven by advanced AI, is displacing traditional jobs at an alarming rate, creating anxiety among workers and reshaping the global economy. Companies that deploy AI solutions must grapple with the ethical implications of their choices: Should they prioritize cost savings over job preservation? How can they support workers whose roles are rendered obsolete by technology? Forward-thinking organizations are embracing strategies to upskill and reskill their workforce, ensuring that employees remain relevant in an AI-driven world. These initiatives not only mitigate the social impact of automation but also foster loyalty and trust among employees, reinforcing the company's reputation as a responsible corporate citizen.

However, the stakeholder revolution extends beyond individual organizations. Governments and regulatory bodies are playing an increasingly active role in defining the boundaries of AI's application, creating a complex landscape of rules and expectations. In some cases, regulations are driving innovation by incentivizing companies to adopt ethical AI practices. The European Union's AI Act, for instance, establishes strict guidelines for high-risk AI systems, pushing organizations to prioritize transparency and accountability. In other cases, regulatory pressure can stifle innovation, as companies struggle to navigate conflicting requirements across jurisdictions. To thrive in this environment, businesses must engage with policymakers, advocating for balanced regulations that promote both innovation and societal well-being.

The interplay between AI and governance also has profound implications for corporate culture. As organizations embrace AI, they must cultivate a culture of ethical vigilance, where employees at all levels feel empowered to question and challenge the use of AI systems. This requires clear communication, robust training programs, and mechanisms for whistleblowing without fear of retaliation. When employees are equipped with the knowledge and tools to understand AI's impact, they become active participants in the governance process, ensuring that the organization's values align with its technological practices.

Perhaps the most significant shift in power dynamics is the growing influence of the public in shaping corporate behavior. Social media platforms, powered by AI algorithms, amplify voices that were once marginalized, creating a global stage for public scrutiny. Companies that fail to act responsibly risk facing viral backlash, boycotts, and reputational damage. Conversely, organizations that demonstrate genuine commitment to ethical AI practices can build trust and loyalty among consumers, turning responsibility into a competitive advantage.

The new power dynamics of AI, governance, and corporate responsibility ultimately challenge organizations to rethink their purpose. In an era where technological capabilities are expanding exponentially, the question is no longer what companies can do with AI, but what they should do. Businesses that rise to this challenge will not only navigate the complexities of the stakeholder revolution but also lead it, setting a standard for innovation, integrity, and impact.

As we look to the future, one thing is clear: AI is not just a tool for enhancing productivity or reducing costs. It is a catalyst for systemic change, reshaping the relationships between organizations, stakeholders, and society at large. The companies that succeed in this new landscape will be those that embrace the power of AI responsibly, leveraging its potential to drive sustainable growth while upholding their commitments to the people and communities they serve. In doing so, they will not only create value but also redefine what it means to be a responsible and forward-thinking organization in the age of AI.

AI and the Stakeholder Revolution: Navigating Controversies in a Rapidly Changing World

In *AI and the Stakeholder Revolution*, we dive into the evolving dynamics between artificial intelligence (AI), corporate decision-making, and stakeholder governance. This transformation isn't just a technological one—it's a cultural shift reshaping how businesses create and destroy value in an era demanding sustainable futures. The growing importance of stakeholder governance—where the interests of employees, communities, and the environment weigh alongside shareholder profits—has collided with the rapid adoption of AI in decision-making. While the possibilities are staggering, they come with significant controversies.

Here are the three key tensions defining this revolution:

---

1. Transparency vs. Competitive Advantage: The Trust Dilemma

AI-powered systems enable unprecedented precision in corporate decision-making, but their complexity often shrouds operations in a "black box" of opacity. Stakeholders—employees, customers, regulators, and communities—demand transparency in AI's operations, yet businesses argue that revealing too much can jeopardize their competitive edge.

The Controversy: Corporations often deploy AI algorithms to optimize decisions, such as determining product pricing, allocating resources, or even predicting consumer behavior. However, stakeholders increasingly demand clarity about these algorithms' fairness and ethical implications. For instance:

- **Employees** question whether AI systems are used to surveil productivity or make hiring decisions.
- **Consumers** ask if AI-powered pricing models exploit vulnerable populations.
- **Regulators** demand explanations for algorithmic decisions that influence access to critical services, like healthcare or housing.

Transparency is ethically and legally important, yet fully revealing how AI systems operate can expose intellectual property or even allow malicious actors to game the system. This trust dilemma becomes acute when companies face backlash for perceived AI misuse, as seen in controversies like biased hiring algorithms or discriminatory loan approvals.

Implications for Decision-Making:

- Companies must find a balance between operational opacity and ethical transparency.
- Building stakeholder trust through third-party audits or explainable AI initiatives can help—but these add costs and require industry-wide collaboration to set standards.

Call to Action: For leaders, embracing radical transparency is not just an ethical imperative but a competitive strategy. Stakeholders reward companies that align AI practices with societal values. Forward-thinking organizations will collaborate on shared frameworks for transparency, enabling AI to benefit both business and society.

2. Efficiency vs. Ethical Responsibility: The Automation Debate

AI promises efficiency through automation, but at what human cost? This is perhaps the most visible tension of the stakeholder revolution: businesses' drive to reduce costs and maximize productivity clashes with their responsibility to protect workers and communities.

The Controversy: Automation enables companies to streamline operations, from customer service chatbots to fully automated factories. However, this technological leap comes with consequences:

- **Mass Job Displacement:** Millions of workers risk losing their livelihoods to AI systems.
- **Widening Inequality:** While some benefit from higher productivity, others—particularly low-skilled workers—face marginalization.
- **Erosion of Human Dignity:** Critics argue that replacing human decision-making with AI in sensitive contexts (e.g., healthcare or justice systems) diminishes the value of empathy and judgment.

Stakeholder governance requires balancing these efficiencies with ethical responsibilities. Yet in practice, corporate actions often prioritize short-term gains over long-term sustainability. For instance:

- Retail giants have faced criticism for replacing human cashiers with self-checkout kiosks, leaving communities with fewer employment opportunities.
- The tech industry continues to develop autonomous systems that make decisions faster and more accurately than humans, but with limited accountability for when those decisions go awry.

Implications for Decision-Making:

- Boards must weigh the benefits of automation against its social costs, crafting strategies that account for worker retraining and community investment.
- Policy frameworks like Universal Basic Income or "robot taxes" may become necessary to address the broader impacts of automation.

Call to Action: Businesses that view automation through a purely economic lens risk backlash from disenfranchised stakeholders. The leaders of the stakeholder revolution must redefine success by integrating worker welfare and community resilience into their AI strategies.

3. Innovation vs. Accountability: Who Bears the Risks?

AI-driven innovation is accelerating at breakneck speed, reshaping industries from healthcare to finance. But as innovation races ahead, accountability often lags, leaving stakeholders vulnerable to unanticipated risks.

The Controversy: AI's potential to disrupt traditional industries creates new opportunities, but it also raises ethical and legal questions:

- **Bias and Discrimination:** AI systems often reflect the biases of their training data, perpetuating inequality in critical domains like hiring or policing.
- **Data Privacy and Security:** With AI relying heavily on data, the risk of misuse or breaches escalates.
- **Unintended Consequences:** Even well-intentioned AI systems can produce harmful outcomes. For instance, an AI model designed to optimize supply chains might recommend environmentally damaging practices.

Accountability becomes murky as companies push boundaries, often with limited oversight. This "move fast and break things" mindset, popularized by Silicon Valley, has led to catastrophic failures—from self-driving car accidents to social media algorithms amplifying misinformation.

Implications for Decision-Making:

- Leaders must establish guardrails for AI innovation, such as ethical review boards or compliance frameworks.
- Policymakers need to keep pace with technological advancements, ensuring that regulations protect stakeholder interests without stifling innovation.

Call to Action: Businesses must proactively own their accountability in the stakeholder revolution. This means not only anticipating risks but also addressing them with agility and transparency. Collaboration between corporations, governments, and civil society is essential to foster innovation while safeguarding the public good.

The relationship between AI, corporate decision-making, and stakeholder governance is complex and fraught with challenges. Yet, these controversies offer an opportunity for forward-thinking leaders to redefine what it means to create value in a rapidly changing world.

To succeed in the stakeholder revolution, companies must embrace:

1. **Transparent Practices:** Opening up AI operations to scrutiny builds trust and mitigates risks.
2. **Ethical Priorities:** Balancing efficiency with humanity ensures long-term sustainability.
3. **Shared Accountability:** Taking collective responsibility for AI's impacts helps navigate uncertainties.

The stakeholder revolution isn't a zero-sum game—it's a chance to create a world where AI drives progress for everyone, not just a privileged few. As businesses reimagine their role in society, they have the power to shape a future that balances innovation with responsibility. The choices made today will echo across generations, defining not just corporate success but humanity's collective legacy.

CHAPTER 4: BALANCING INNOVATION AND INCLUSION

Innovation is the lifeblood of modern enterprise. In the AI-driven economy, companies that fail to innovate risk becoming irrelevant. Yet, as organizations sprint toward the future, they often overlook a critical question:

Who is being left behind? This chapter explores how leaders can balance the drive for cutting-edge progress with the imperative to ensure inclusivity for all stakeholders.

The Double-Edged Sword of Innovation

Innovation brings immense opportunities: new markets, revolutionary products, and transformative efficiencies. But it also disrupts industries, eliminates jobs, and can deepen existing inequalities. For example, consider the rise of automation. While some companies saw profits soar through streamlined operations, entire communities were devastated by job displacement.

The challenge for today's leaders isn't just to innovate—it's to innovate responsibly. This means understanding not only how new technologies create value but also how they may inadvertently destroy it for certain groups.

The Inclusion Imperative

At its core, inclusion is about ensuring that everyone, regardless of their background, benefits from innovation. Organizations embracing this mindset are doing more than ticking a box; they're investing in long-term resilience.

Case Study: Tech and Accessibility

Consider a leading tech firm that developed an AI-powered app to help individuals with visual impairments navigate the world. By designing with inclusion in mind, the company opened up new markets while addressing a real societal need. The lesson? Inclusive innovation isn't just ethical—it's profitable.

A Framework for Inclusive Innovation

1. **Engage Stakeholders Early**
   Involve employees, customers, and community members in the innovation process. These groups can provide valuable insights about potential impacts—positive and negative.

   "We didn't just design for our users; we designed with them," said a product manager from a health-tech startup whose user-centered approach led to a 300% increase in customer retention.

2. **Leverage Diverse Teams**
   Research shows that diverse teams outperform homogenous ones, especially in solving complex problems. Leaders should cultivate diversity not only as a moral imperative but also as a strategic advantage.
3. **Adopt a Long-Term Perspective**
   Balancing short-term profitability with long-term societal impact is challenging but essential. Companies that prioritize sustainable growth often enjoy stronger brand loyalty and reduced regulatory risks.

The Risks of Ignoring Inclusion

Innovation without inclusion risks public backlash, legal challenges, and reputational damage. Remember when a major tech company faced boycotts after their facial recognition software exhibited racial bias? They had rushed to market without adequately testing for inclusivity, costing them millions in lost contracts and trust.

The Future of Stakeholder-Centric Innovation

In a world increasingly driven by AI and rapid technological change, balancing innovation and inclusion is not a "nice to have"—it's a necessity. Companies that master this balance will be the ones creating value that endures.

As you turn the page, we'll explore how these principles are applied in real-world settings, from boardrooms to factory floors. Innovation doesn't have to come at the expense of inclusion. When done right, it creates a world where everyone can thrive.

Aligning Technological Advancement with Equitable Outcomes

The rise of technological advancement has revolutionized every facet of human life—from the way we communicate to the systems powering global economies. Yet, this unrelenting pursuit of innovation poses significant risks to equity. As artificial intelligence, automation, and digital platforms reshape industries, it becomes imperative for organizations to balance progress with the broader societal and environmental impacts of their actions. Failing to do so not only jeopardizes the stability of communities but also risks alienating customers, eroding trust, and damaging ecosystems. This section delves into three significant threats arising from unbalanced technological progress and explores strategies to align innovation with equitable outcomes for employees, customers, communities, and the environment.

Threat 1: Workforce Displacement Through Automation

One of the most pressing consequences of technological advancement is the displacement of workers. Automation and AI have become powerful tools for efficiency, reducing costs, and driving innovation. Yet, these gains often come at the expense of human labor. Entire sectors, particularly manufacturing, logistics, and customer service, face significant job losses due to the widespread adoption of robotics and algorithms capable of replacing repetitive tasks.

The loss of stable employment has cascading effects. Families lose their primary sources of income, communities that rely on specific industries see economic downturns, and the gap between skilled and unskilled workers widens. Moreover, the psychological toll of job displacement—stress, anxiety, and a sense of obsolescence—often goes unaddressed, compounding the societal impact.

Strategies to Address Workforce Displacement

1. **Invest in Reskilling and Upskilling Programs**
   Organizations must take proactive steps to retrain employees whose jobs are at risk. Investing in lifelong learning programs enables workers to transition to roles requiring more advanced skills, particularly in areas like data analysis, programming, or human-centric services that machines cannot replicate. For example, Amazon's *Upskilling 2025* initiative offers employees training in high-demand fields, ensuring they remain competitive in the evolving job market.

2. **Collaborate with Governments and Educational Institutions**
   Partnerships between corporations, governments, and academia can accelerate reskilling efforts. Joint initiatives, such as tax incentives for companies that provide training or public-private programs in technical education, create a safety net for affected workers.

3. **Embrace Human-Machine Collaboration**
   Instead of replacing workers entirely, businesses should explore opportunities to augment human capabilities with technology. Roles that combine human intuition with machine efficiency—such as medical diagnostics or advanced manufacturing—are less likely to result in displacement and foster innovation alongside job creation.

Threat 2: Widening Inequality Among Customers and Communities

As technology evolves, access to its benefits remains unevenly distributed. Affluent populations often gain first access to new innovations, such as advanced healthcare, high-speed internet, and personalized AI-driven services. Meanwhile, underprivileged communities face barriers to adoption due to cost, lack of infrastructure, or limited digital literacy.

This digital divide exacerbates existing inequalities, denying marginalized groups the tools they need to participate in modern economies. For example, in rural areas without reliable internet access, children miss out on online education opportunities, small businesses struggle to compete, and individuals lack access to telehealth services. As a result, technological advancement risks entrenching systemic inequities.

Strategies to Foster Equitable Access

1. **Promote Universal Access to Infrastructure**
   Governments and corporations must prioritize expanding essential digital infrastructure to underserved regions. Partnerships with telecommunications providers to offer subsidized broadband in rural areas or low-income neighborhoods can bridge the digital divide. For instance, Google's *Project Loon*

used high-altitude balloons to deliver internet to remote areas, demonstrating innovative approaches to inclusivity.
2. **Design Affordable Solutions**
Companies can create tiered pricing models or develop low-cost versions of their products tailored to underserved markets. For example, mobile phone manufacturers have launched affordable smartphones with essential features, enabling millions in developing countries to join the digital revolution.
3. **Enhance Digital Literacy**
Access alone is insufficient if individuals cannot use the technology effectively. Corporations should invest in programs that teach digital skills, particularly in marginalized communities. Initiatives like Microsoft's global digital literacy curriculum help empower users to harness technology for education, entrepreneurship, and personal growth.

Threat 3: Environmental Degradation and Resource Exploitation

The rapid pace of technological advancement has often ignored its environmental costs. From the energy-intensive demands of data centers to the extraction of rare minerals for electronic devices, the tech industry contributes significantly to ecological harm. Left unchecked, these practices jeopardize the planet's health, disproportionately impacting vulnerable populations who rely on natural ecosystems for their livelihoods.

For example, e-waste—the discarded components of obsolete technology—poses a growing crisis. Toxic materials leach into soil and water, affecting communities in developing nations where much of this waste is improperly disposed. Additionally, the proliferation of energy-intensive technologies, such as cryptocurrency mining, strains power grids and accelerates climate change.

Strategies to Mitigate Environmental Impact
1. **Adopt Circular Economy Principles**
Transitioning to a circular economy—where products are designed for reuse, recycling, and minimal waste—can significantly reduce environmental harm. Tech companies should prioritize modular designs that allow devices to be repaired or upgraded, reducing the need for new resource extraction. Apple's commitment to using 100% recycled aluminum in its products sets an example of how sustainable practices can align with profitability.
2. **Invest in Renewable Energy**
Data centers and manufacturing facilities can transition to renewable energy sources, such as solar or wind power, to minimize carbon footprints. Companies like Google and Amazon have pledged to run their operations on 100% renewable energy, demonstrating the feasibility of sustainable tech infrastructure.
3. **Implement Responsible Supply Chains**
Organizations must ensure that raw materials are sourced ethically and sustainably. Collaborating with suppliers to improve labor practices, reduce

environmental damage, and increase transparency across the supply chain is critical. Certifications such as Fairtrade or Responsible Minerals Assurance help ensure compliance with ethical standards.

The Holistic Vision: Integrating Stakeholders in Innovation

Aligning technological progress with equitable outcomes requires a shift in mindset. Instead of viewing innovation solely through the lens of profitability or efficiency, organizations must adopt a stakeholder-centric approach that prioritizes people and the planet alongside financial performance.

1. **Embed Equity into Decision-Making Frameworks**
   Equity should not be an afterthought but a core component of every strategic decision. Companies can establish cross-functional committees that assess the societal and environmental impacts of new technologies, ensuring that innovation aligns with the broader good.

2. **Emphasize Transparent Communication**
   Building trust requires transparency. Regularly communicating the steps taken to address inequality or environmental impact fosters goodwill among employees, customers, and communities. Public accountability through sustainability reports or independent audits helps ensure progress.

3. **Collaborate Across Sectors**
   Solving systemic challenges demands collective action. Partnerships between corporations, governments, and non-profits can amplify impact. For example, the *Tech for Good* initiative brings together companies to tackle global challenges such as climate change and digital equity, pooling resources and expertise for greater results.

The rapid pace of technological advancement holds incredible promise but also profound risks. Left unchecked, innovation can exacerbate workforce displacement, deepen social inequalities, and accelerate environmental degradation. However, with thoughtful strategies and a commitment to equitable outcomes, organizations can ensure that progress benefits all stakeholders.

By investing in reskilling, expanding digital access, and adopting sustainable practices, leaders can create a future where employees thrive in new roles, customers enjoy inclusive access to innovation, communities prosper, and ecosystems are preserved. The journey toward equitable technological advancement demands vision, collaboration, and accountability—but the rewards of a just and sustainable world are well worth the effort.

Threat	Description	Strategies for Alignment
Workforce Displacement	Job losses due to automation and AI replacing repetitive tasks.	1. Invest in reskilling and upskilling programs. 2. Collaborate with governments and academia for retraining initiatives. 3. Promote human-machine collaboration.
Widening Inequality	Unequal access to technological benefits, disadvantaging marginalized groups.	1. Expand digital infrastructure in underserved areas. 2. Offer affordable, inclusive solutions. 3. Enhance digital literacy programs.
Environmental Degradation	Ecological harm from resource exploitation, e-waste, and energy-intensive tech.	1. Adopt circular economy practices to reduce waste. 2. Transition to renewable energy sources. 3. Ensure responsible, sustainable supply chains.

CHAPTER 5: FUTURE-PROOFING ORGANIZATIONS IN A RAPIDLY CHANGING WORLD

In an era characterized by unprecedented technological advancements, global interconnectivity, and shifting societal expectations, organizations face the daunting challenge of remaining relevant and competitive. The rapid pace of change in today's world has made it clear that traditional approaches to organizational strategy, leadership, and decision-making are no longer sufficient. Companies that fail to adapt risk being displaced by agile competitors, disrupted by technological innovation, or abandoned by stakeholders whose values no longer align with outdated practices. This chapter delves into the principles and strategies that can help organizations future-proof themselves, ensuring they not only survive but thrive in an ever-changing environment.

Understanding the Dynamics of Change

Change has always been a part of the business landscape, but the current velocity and complexity of transformation are unparalleled. This acceleration is driven by the convergence of several forces: technological disruption, globalization, climate change, and shifting consumer and employee expectations.

Technological innovation, particularly in the realms of artificial intelligence (AI), automation, and data analytics, has fundamentally reshaped how businesses operate. Processes once considered essential are being rendered obsolete, while entirely new business models emerge. For example, the advent of AI-driven decision-making has created opportunities for unprecedented efficiency but has also raised ethical concerns around transparency and fairness.

Globalization, though challenged by geopolitical tensions, continues to drive interdependence among markets. Supply chain disruptions during the COVID-19 pandemic highlighted the fragility of global systems while reinforcing the need for resilience and adaptability.

Environmental imperatives, including the need to address climate change, have become central to business strategy. Organizations are increasingly held accountable for their environmental impact by governments, investors, and consumers. Sustainable practices are no longer optional—they are essential to maintaining a license to operate.

Finally, stakeholder expectations have shifted dramatically. Employees demand meaningful work, consumers favor socially responsible brands, and investors increasingly prioritize Environmental, Social, and Governance (ESG) factors. The rise of the stakeholder economy means organizations must balance profitability with broader societal impact.

The Risks of Inertia

Organizations that resist change are at significant risk of obsolescence. The failure to anticipate or respond to evolving dynamics can lead to market share erosion, reputational damage, and financial collapse. Blockbuster's decline in the face of Netflix's rise is a cautionary tale of what happens when companies fail to adapt to technological innovation and changing consumer habits. Similarly, the collapse of major retailers that ignored the shift to e-commerce underscores the perils of inertia.

Inertia often stems from deeply ingrained cultural norms, rigid hierarchical structures, and a reluctance to challenge the status quo. Many organizations operate with a short-term focus, prioritizing quarterly earnings over long-term sustainability. This myopia can prevent leaders from recognizing emerging threats or opportunities until it is too late.

The Foundation of Future-Proofing: Agility and Resilience

Future-proofing organizations require a dual focus on agility and resilience. While agility enables rapid adaptation to change, resilience ensures that companies can withstand and recover from disruptions.

Agility: Agility is about speed, flexibility, and responsiveness. Agile organizations are not only quick to respond to change but also proactive in identifying trends and opportunities. This requires a culture of experimentation and a willingness to embrace risk. Companies like Amazon and Tesla have demonstrated the power of agility by continuously innovating and staying ahead of competitors.

To foster agility, organizations should adopt flat structures that facilitate collaboration and decision-making. Bureaucratic processes must be streamlined, and employees should be empowered to act autonomously within a clear strategic framework. Emphasizing cross-functional teams can help break down silos and promote a more dynamic approach to problem-solving.

Resilience: Resilience, on the other hand, is the capacity to endure and adapt in the face of adversity. The COVID-19 pandemic highlighted the importance of resilience as businesses navigated unprecedented disruptions to supply chains, workforce dynamics, and consumer behavior. Resilient organizations anticipate potential disruptions and build contingencies into their operations.

This involves diversifying supply chains, investing in robust digital infrastructure, and fostering a culture of adaptability. Scenario planning and stress testing can help organizations prepare for a range of possibilities, from economic downturns to natural disasters. Resilience is also deeply tied to the mental and emotional well-being of employees, making investments in workplace culture and support systems essential.

Leveraging Technology for Strategic Advantage

Technology plays a pivotal role in future-proofing organizations. AI, machine learning, and data analytics offer powerful tools for enhancing decision-making, improving efficiency, and driving innovation. However, the strategic implementation of technology requires careful consideration of both opportunities and risks.

Harnessing Data: Data is often described as the "new oil," but its value lies in how it is used. Organizations must develop the capacity to collect, analyze, and act on data insights. This involves investing in advanced analytics platforms and ensuring that employees have the skills to leverage these tools effectively.

Automating Processes: Automation can drive significant efficiency gains by eliminating repetitive tasks and reducing human error. However, it also raises concerns about workforce displacement. To future-proof their operations, organizations must strike a balance between automation and human capital, prioritizing upskilling and redeployment of workers.

Fostering Innovation: Technology should be seen as an enabler of innovation rather than a substitute for strategic thinking. Companies must create environments where experimentation and creativity thrive. This involves investing in research and development, encouraging intrapreneurship, and maintaining an openness to external partnerships.

The Role of Leadership in Driving Transformation

Leadership is critical to future-proofing organizations. Leaders must embody a vision of adaptability and inclusivity, setting the tone for cultural and strategic transformation. This involves not only technical competence but also emotional intelligence and the ability to inspire trust.

Visionary Leadership: Effective leaders anticipate change and articulate a compelling vision for the future. They are not afraid to challenge conventional thinking and make bold decisions in the face of uncertainty. Visionary leaders also prioritize purpose, ensuring that their organizations contribute positively to society while achieving financial success.

Inclusive Leadership: Inclusivity is essential to harnessing diverse perspectives and driving innovation. Leaders must create environments where all voices are heard and valued. This involves addressing unconscious bias, fostering a culture of psychological safety, and actively seeking input from a broad range of stakeholders.

Transformational Leadership: Transformational leaders go beyond managing change—they actively shape it. They empower employees, build high-performing teams, and cultivate a sense of ownership and accountability across the organization. By leading with authenticity and empathy, they inspire employees to embrace change as an opportunity rather than a threat.

Embedding a Stakeholder-Centric Approach

Future-proofing organizations requires a fundamental shift from shareholder primacy to stakeholder inclusivity. This involves balancing the needs of employees, customers, investors, communities, and the environment. Companies that adopt a stakeholder-centric approach are better positioned to navigate change and build long-term resilience.

Employee Engagement: Employees are a company's greatest asset. Engaged employees are more productive, innovative, and committed to their organization's success. Future-proofing requires creating meaningful work experiences, offering opportunities for growth, and prioritizing well-being. Transparent communication and a strong sense of purpose can also foster loyalty and motivation.

Customer Focus: Understanding and anticipating customer needs is critical to remaining competitive. This involves leveraging data to gain insights into consumer behavior, preferences, and values. Companies that align their offerings with societal trends—such as sustainability and ethical sourcing—can build lasting customer loyalty.

Environmental Stewardship: Climate change and environmental degradation pose existential threats to businesses and society. Future-proofing organizations must prioritize sustainability, reducing their carbon footprint and adopting circular economy principles.

Transparent reporting on ESG metrics can enhance credibility and attract socially conscious investors.

Future-proofing is not a one-time effort—it is an ongoing process of adaptation and renewal. Organizations must cultivate a mindset of continuous learning, remaining attuned to emerging trends and proactively addressing challenges. This requires investment in people, processes, and technologies, as well as a commitment to purpose-driven leadership.

While the path forward is uncertain, the principles outlined in this chapter provide a roadmap for navigating complexity and change. By embracing agility, resilience, technological innovation, and stakeholder inclusivity, organizations can position themselves for sustained success in a rapidly changing world. Future-proofing is not just about surviving disruption—it is about creating value in the face of it.

Practical Approaches for Leveraging AI to Build Resilient, Adaptive Organizations That Thrive Amidst Uncertainty

In the modern business landscape, uncertainty has become the new normal. From economic instability to rapid technological advancements and global disruptions such as pandemics and climate change, organizations face an increasingly unpredictable future. To navigate this complexity, many are turning to artificial intelligence (AI) as a cornerstone for building resilience and adaptability. However, the promise of AI is accompanied by challenges that require strategic approaches to implementation and integration.

This chapter explores three principal challenges organizations face when leveraging AI to foster resilience and adaptability, along with practical approaches to overcome these hurdles. By addressing these challenges, businesses can unlock the transformative potential of AI, ensuring they not only survive but thrive in an uncertain world.

Challenge 1: Bridging the Gap Between Data and Decision-Making

One of the most significant challenges in leveraging AI effectively is the disconnect between the vast amounts of data available to organizations and their ability to translate that data into actionable insights. While AI excels at processing and analyzing data, its true value lies in empowering decision-makers to act with precision and confidence. Yet, many organizations struggle to fully utilize AI due to data silos, poor data quality, and insufficient alignment between AI insights and strategic goals.

Practical Approaches:

1. **Data Infrastructure Modernization**
   A foundational step in harnessing AI is establishing a robust data infrastructure. This involves breaking down silos, ensuring interoperability across systems, and investing in cloud-based solutions for scalability. Modern data lakes and warehouses enable organizations to consolidate diverse datasets, making them accessible to AI models. Furthermore, implementing tools that automate data cleaning and preparation ensures high-quality inputs, a critical factor in generating reliable AI outputs.

2. **Building Decision-Centric AI Models**
   Rather than overwhelming leadership with excessive data, organizations should focus on designing AI systems that provide clear, actionable recommendations. This requires collaboration between data scientists, business analysts, and decision-makers to define key performance indicators (KPIs) and decision thresholds. By tailoring AI outputs to align with strategic goals, businesses can bridge the gap between data and decision-making.
3. **Fostering a Data-Literate Culture**
   Data literacy across the workforce is essential to maximizing the value of AI. Organizations should invest in training programs that empower employees to interpret AI-driven insights and integrate them into their workflows. Building a culture where data-driven decision-making is the norm creates an environment in which AI thrives as a tool for strategic guidance.
4. **Human-AI Collaboration Frameworks**
   Successful AI adoption requires clear delineation of roles between human decision-makers and AI systems. Organizations must identify scenarios where AI serves as a complement to human intuition and where it acts as the primary driver of decisions. For instance, while AI can rapidly analyze risk scenarios, humans should remain responsible for decisions that require ethical considerations or nuanced judgment.

Challenge 2: Mitigating Bias and Ethical Risks in AI Systems

As organizations integrate AI into critical processes, they must confront the challenge of bias and ethical risks inherent in these systems. AI algorithms are only as good as the data they are trained on, and biased datasets can perpetuate discrimination, inequity, or flawed decision-making. Furthermore, the opaque nature of many AI models—often referred to as the "black box" problem—makes it difficult to explain or justify outcomes, which can undermine trust.

Practical Approaches:

1. **Bias Auditing and Inclusive Data Practices**
   Mitigating bias begins with rigorous auditing of datasets to ensure they are representative and free from harmful stereotypes. Organizations should adopt inclusive data collection practices, ensuring diverse inputs that reflect the full spectrum of their stakeholders. Regular testing of AI outputs for disparate impacts can help identify and address bias early in the development process.
2. **Ethical AI Frameworks**
   Establishing a clear ethical framework for AI is crucial to maintaining trust and accountability. This involves defining principles such as fairness, transparency, and accountability and embedding them into AI development and deployment processes. Many organizations are appointing ethics boards or AI ethics officers to oversee compliance with these principles.
3. **Explainable AI (XAI)**
   To enhance transparency, organizations should prioritize the development of

explainable AI systems. XAI techniques allow users to understand the rationale behind an AI's decision, increasing trust and enabling more effective oversight. For example, decision trees or rule-based models can provide clear reasoning for outputs, while visualization tools can help stakeholders explore data relationships.
4. **Human Oversight and Intervention**
   Embedding human oversight into AI systems is essential for ethical risk mitigation. Organizations should implement mechanisms for flagging and reviewing high-stakes decisions made by AI, ensuring that human judgment remains a safeguard against potential errors or biases.
5. **Regulatory and Compliance Alignment**
   The regulatory landscape for AI is rapidly evolving, with governments and international bodies introducing guidelines to ensure ethical AI use. Organizations must stay abreast of these developments and ensure compliance with relevant regulations. Proactive engagement with policymakers can also position businesses as leaders in ethical AI adoption.

Challenge 3: Ensuring Scalability and Integration Across the Organization

A common stumbling block in leveraging AI is the difficulty of scaling and integrating AI capabilities across diverse business functions. While pilot projects often demonstrate promising results, transitioning from isolated applications to organization-wide implementation presents significant challenges. Factors such as resistance to change, misaligned objectives, and technical incompatibilities can hinder progress.

Practical Approaches:
1. **Strategic Alignment with Business Goals**
   For AI to scale effectively, its applications must align with the organization's strategic objectives. Leaders should identify high-impact use cases where AI can drive measurable value, such as improving operational efficiency, enhancing customer experience, or enabling predictive maintenance. Clear alignment ensures that AI initiatives receive the necessary resources and support.
2. **Adopting Scalable AI Platforms**
   Many organizations struggle to scale AI due to reliance on disparate tools and systems. Investing in unified AI platforms that integrate with existing IT infrastructure can streamline deployment and management. These platforms should offer modular capabilities, allowing businesses to scale AI incrementally as their needs evolve.
3. **Change Management and Employee Buy-In**
   Resistance to change is a significant barrier to scaling AI. To address this, organizations must prioritize change management, involving employees at all levels in the AI journey. Transparent communication about the benefits of AI, coupled with opportunities for hands-on engagement, can build trust and enthusiasm.

4. **Cross-Functional Collaboration**
   Scaling AI requires collaboration across departments, from IT and operations to marketing and HR. Establishing cross-functional teams that bring together diverse expertise ensures that AI initiatives are designed and implemented with a holistic perspective. This collaborative approach also facilitates knowledge sharing and best practices.
5. **Continuous Monitoring and Improvement**
   AI systems require ongoing refinement to remain effective. Organizations should establish feedback loops that monitor performance, identify areas for improvement, and adapt models as conditions change. Continuous learning ensures that AI systems evolve in tandem with the organization's needs and the external environment.

The Path Forward: Building a Resilient, AI-Driven Organization

The transformative potential of AI lies not in its ability to replace human intelligence but in its capacity to augment and enhance it. By addressing the challenges of data integration, ethical risks, and scalability, organizations can harness AI as a powerful tool for resilience and adaptability. Success requires a strategic, human-centered approach that prioritizes collaboration, ethical responsibility, and alignment with long-term goals.

In a world of uncertainty, AI offers a competitive edge for organizations willing to invest in its potential and navigate its complexities. Those that embrace this journey will find themselves not just surviving disruption but leading the way in shaping the future. By leveraging AI effectively, businesses can build adaptive systems, foster innovation, and create enduring value for their stakeholders.

APPENDICES

APPENDIX 1: AI GOVERNANCE FRAMEWORKS: A GUIDE FOR LEADERS

As artificial intelligence (AI) becomes a cornerstone of modern business, implementing robust governance frameworks is critical to aligning AI's potential with stakeholder interests. This appendix provides practical tools, checklists, and real-world examples to help leaders craft AI governance structures that foster accountability, transparency, and ethical use.

Why AI Governance Matters

AI systems influence decision-making across industries, impacting employees, customers, communities, and the environment. Without proper governance, these systems can lead to unintended consequences, from biased algorithms to unchecked environmental costs. Establishing a governance framework ensures that AI aligns with organizational values and stakeholder expectations.

Key Components of an AI Governance Framework

1. Accountability Structures

- **Designated AI Ethics Board:** Form a cross-functional team including technologists, ethicists, legal advisors, and representatives from diverse stakeholder groups.
- **Executive Ownership:** Assign C-level responsibility for AI governance, such as a Chief AI Officer or Chief Ethics Officer.
- **Reporting Lines:** Establish clear lines of accountability, ensuring that AI-related decisions and concerns are escalated appropriately.

2. Transparency Mechanisms

- **Algorithmic Explainability:** Use models and tools that provide clear explanations for AI-driven decisions.
- **Stakeholder Communication:** Regularly publish AI impact reports, detailing system objectives, methodologies, and outcomes.
- **Audit Trails:** Implement robust documentation to track AI system design, training, and deployment processes.

3. Ethical Risk Management

- **Bias Detection and Mitigation:** Regularly audit data sets and algorithms for biases and inequities.
- **Environmental Responsibility:** Evaluate the energy consumption of AI processes and invest in greener alternatives when possible.
- **Human Oversight:** Design systems that allow humans to intervene or override decisions in high-stakes scenarios.

4. Compliance and Legal Alignment

- Align AI practices with local and international laws, including data privacy regulations (e.g., GDPR, CCPA).
- Monitor emerging legal frameworks for AI governance and adapt policies proactively.

Practical Tools for AI Governance

AI Governance Checklist

- **Risk Assessment:** Have you identified and assessed all potential risks associated with AI deployment?
- **Stakeholder Inclusion:** Are stakeholder perspectives incorporated into AI design and governance processes?

- **Transparency:** Are the AI system's decision-making processes explainable to non-technical stakeholders?
- **Bias Management:** Have data and algorithms been audited for fairness?
- **Compliance:** Are AI activities compliant with all applicable laws and ethical standards?

Governance Templates

- **Ethical Review Template:** A document outlining questions and metrics for evaluating AI projects from an ethical standpoint.
- **Incident Response Plan:** A predefined protocol for addressing unintended AI consequences.

Examples of Effective AI Governance

Case 1: Company A – Building Stakeholder Trust through Transparency

A global healthcare provider implemented an AI governance framework emphasizing transparency. By publishing clear algorithmic decision-making processes and hosting public forums to address concerns, the company increased trust among patients, regulators, and employees.

Case 2: Company B – Environmental Stewardship

A tech firm optimized its AI systems to reduce energy consumption by 40%, incorporating renewable energy sources for training large models. This initiative not only aligned with sustainability goals but also attracted environmentally conscious investors.

Steps to Implement AI Governance

1. **Conduct a Governance Audit:** Assess existing policies and gaps in AI oversight.
2. **Engage Stakeholders:** Organize workshops to gather insights from affected groups.
3. **Pilot Programs:** Begin with small-scale implementation of governance measures to refine processes.
4. **Measure and Iterate:** Regularly review governance frameworks and update them to adapt to new challenges and technologies.

APPENDIX 2: CASE STUDIES – COMPANIES THRIVING AND FAILING IN THE STAKEHOLDER REVOLUTION

In this appendix, we examine real-world case studies of companies that have successfully navigated the stakeholder revolution with AI, as well as those that have faltered. These examples highlight critical lessons in balancing stakeholder priorities with AI innovation.

Success Stories

Case Study 1: Thriving with AI-Driven Employee Empowerment

Company: RetailTech Co.

Context: RetailTech Co., a multinational retailer, faced challenges managing workforce productivity and satisfaction across its global stores.

AI Implementation:
The company deployed AI systems to optimize employee schedules, ensuring fair workloads while accommodating personal preferences. Additionally, AI-powered training modules personalized learning paths, enabling employees to upskill effectively.

Outcome:
- **Employee Satisfaction:** Workforce satisfaction scores rose by 35% within the first year.
- **Operational Efficiency:** Productivity increased by 20%, driven by happier, more engaged employees.
- **Reputation:** The company was recognized for its employee-first approach, strengthening its employer brand.

Key Takeaway: AI solutions that prioritize stakeholder well-being can simultaneously enhance business outcomes.

Case Study 2: Sustainable AI in Action

Company: AgroAI Solutions

Context: AgroAI Solutions, a startup in the agricultural sector, sought to address food insecurity while minimizing environmental impact.

AI Implementation:
Using predictive analytics, the company developed systems to optimize crop yields while reducing resource consumption. AI-driven monitoring systems provided farmers with real-time insights, enabling precise irrigation and fertilization.

Outcome:
- **Environmental Impact:** Water usage decreased by 30%, and fertilizer application was reduced by 25%.
- **Community Impact:** Farmers reported higher incomes due to increased yields and lower costs.
- **Global Recognition:** The company gained international acclaim for advancing sustainable agriculture.

Key Takeaway: AI can be a transformative force when integrated into strategies that balance economic, social, and environmental goals.

Pitfalls and Failures
Case Study 3: Ignoring Stakeholder Concerns
Company: FinTechX
Context: FinTechX, a financial technology startup, developed AI algorithms to assess loan eligibility quickly.
AI Implementation:
While the system drastically reduced loan approval times, it relied on biased historical data that disproportionately disadvantaged minority groups.
Outcome:
- **Stakeholder Backlash:** The company faced lawsuits and public criticism for perpetuating systemic inequalities.
- **Regulatory Action:** Authorities imposed fines and mandated extensive audits.
- **Business Impact:** Customer trust eroded, leading to a significant drop in market share.

Key Takeaway: AI systems trained on biased data can exacerbate inequalities, leading to reputational and financial losses.

Case Study 4: Overlooking Environmental Costs
Company: MegaAI Tech
Context: MegaAI Tech, a leader in AI research, developed large-scale models requiring vast computational resources.
AI Implementation:
The company's AI training processes consumed enormous amounts of energy, significantly increasing its carbon footprint. Despite warnings, sustainability concerns were deprioritized in favor of speed and scalability.
Outcome:
- **Public Outcry:** Environmental groups campaigned against the company's unsustainable practices.
- **Investor Pullout:** ESG-focused investors divested, citing misalignment with sustainability principles.
- **Market Decline:** The company's reputation as an innovator was overshadowed by its environmental negligence.

Key Takeaway: Ignoring environmental sustainability in AI development can lead to reputational damage and lost investment opportunities.

Lessons Learned from Successes and Failures
1. Balance Stakeholder Priorities
AI initiatives must consider the diverse needs of stakeholders, from employees and customers to investors and the broader community.

2. Prioritize Transparency
Clear communication about AI's purpose, functionality, and impact fosters trust and mitigates backlash.

3. Monitor and Adapt
Continuous monitoring and iterative improvement are essential for maintaining alignment with stakeholder expectations.

4. Think Long-Term

Short-term gains from cutting corners in ethics or sustainability often lead to long-term losses in reputation and trust.

5. Embrace Collaboration

Involving diverse perspectives in AI design and governance leads to more equitable and effective outcomes.

APPENDIX 3: AI ETHICS: PRINCIPLES, POLICIES, AND PITFALLS

As AI transforms industries, the ethical considerations surrounding its use have become more critical. This appendix explores the foundational principles of AI ethics, the policies organizations are adopting to operationalize them, and the common pitfalls businesses face in aligning AI development with ethical standards.

Principles of AI Ethics

1. Fairness and Inclusion

AI systems must be designed to treat all individuals equitably, avoiding discrimination based on race, gender, socioeconomic status, or other protected characteristics.

- **Key Challenge:** Addressing biases inherent in historical data that can lead to discriminatory outcomes.
- **Example:** An AI hiring tool trained on biased data may systematically disadvantage certain groups.

2. Transparency and Explainability

AI systems should be understandable to stakeholders. Users and impacted parties need clarity on how decisions are made.

- **Practical Implementation:** Organizations can use "white-box" AI models where decision-making processes are interpretable, instead of "black-box" models that obscure internal logic.

3. Accountability

Developers and organizations must take responsibility for AI outcomes, including unintended consequences.

- **Example:** If an autonomous vehicle causes an accident, clarity is needed on who holds liability — the manufacturer, programmer, or operator.

4. Privacy and Data Security

AI systems must respect individuals' privacy rights and safeguard sensitive information.

- **Emerging Trend:** Adopting privacy-enhancing technologies like federated learning to minimize risks while enabling innovation.

5. Sustainability

Organizations must consider the environmental impact of AI, particularly energy-intensive training processes for large models.

Policies to Operationalize AI Ethics

1. Ethical AI Guidelines

Organizations are developing internal policies to govern ethical AI use.

- **Example:** Google's AI Principles emphasize socially beneficial applications and prohibit the creation of AI weapons.

2. Third-Party Audits

Independent evaluations help ensure compliance with ethical standards.

- **Benefits:** Builds stakeholder trust and mitigates risks of reputational damage.

3. Ethics Training Programs

Educating employees on ethical AI ensures they recognize and address potential issues in their work.

Pitfalls in Ethical AI

1. Ignoring Long-Term Consequences

Focusing solely on short-term gains can lead to ethical missteps, such as deploying AI systems without adequate testing.

2. Superficial Commitment to Ethics

Some organizations engage in "ethics washing," making public commitments without substantive action.

- **Red Flags:** Vague policies, lack of accountability structures, and absence of stakeholder engagement.

3. Overlooking Marginalized Communities

AI systems designed without considering diverse perspectives risk reinforcing inequalities.

- **Case in Point:** Language models trained predominantly on English data may perform poorly in other languages, disadvantaging non-English speakers.

Regulatory Trends in AI Ethics

Governments and international organizations are shaping the regulatory landscape for AI ethics.

- **EU's AI Act:** Proposes a risk-based classification of AI systems, with strict requirements for high-risk applications like healthcare and law enforcement.
- **US AI Bill of Rights Blueprint:** Outlines principles for protecting civil rights in AI applications.
- **UNESCO's AI Ethics Recommendation:** Provides a global framework for responsible AI use.

APPENDIX 4: GLOSSARY OF TERMS AND KEY CONCEPTS IN AI AND STAKEHOLDER STRATEGY

This glossary provides a comprehensive guide to the terminology and ideas central to understanding AI and stakeholder strategies in the modern business landscape.

Key AI Terms

1. Algorithm

A set of instructions designed to solve a specific problem or perform a task.

2. Artificial Intelligence (AI)

The simulation of human intelligence by machines, including learning (machine learning), reasoning, and self-correction.

3. Bias in AI

Systematic errors in AI outcomes caused by skewed data or flawed algorithms, often leading to unfair treatment of certain groups.

4. Black-Box AI

AI models whose internal workings are opaque, making it difficult to understand how decisions are made.

5. Deep Learning

A subset of machine learning that uses neural networks with many layers to analyze data and identify patterns.

6. Federated Learning

A privacy-preserving method where AI models are trained across decentralized devices using local data, without sharing sensitive information.

7. Natural Language Processing (NLP)

The branch of AI focused on enabling machines to understand, interpret, and respond to human language.

8. Neural Network

A computational model inspired by the structure of the human brain, used in machine learning for recognizing patterns and making predictions.

Key Stakeholder Strategy Terms

1. Stakeholder Capitalism

A business philosophy emphasizing value creation for all stakeholders, including employees, customers, communities, and the environment, rather than focusing solely on shareholders.

2. ESG (Environmental, Social, and Governance)

A framework for evaluating an organization's sustainability and ethical impact.

3. Materiality Assessment

A process for identifying and prioritizing ESG issues that are most relevant to an organization's stakeholders.

4. Triple Bottom Line

A framework considering three dimensions of performance: financial, social, and environmental.

5. Impact Investing

Investing with the intention of generating measurable social and environmental impact alongside financial returns.

APPENDIX 5: RESOURCES FOR FURTHER LEARNING

To deepen your understanding of AI, stakeholder capitalism, and responsible innovation, this appendix provides a curated list of books, articles, and online resources.

Recommended Books

AI and Technology

1. **"Artificial Intelligence: A Guide to Intelligent Systems"** by Michael Negnevitsky
   A foundational text exploring AI principles and practical applications.
2. **"Weapons of Math Destruction"** by Cathy O'Neil
   A critique of the societal impacts of biased algorithms and big data.
3. **"Prediction Machines: The Simple Economics of Artificial Intelligence"** by Ajay Agrawal, Joshua Gans, and Avi Goldfarb
   An accessible exploration of AI's economic implications.

Stakeholder Capitalism

1. **"Stakeholder Capitalism"** by Klaus Schwab
   An argument for rethinking capitalism to prioritize long-term value creation for all stakeholders.
2. **"Conscious Capitalism"** by John Mackey and Raj Sisodia
   Insights on how businesses can thrive while prioritizing ethical practices and stakeholder well-being.

Ethics and Governance

1. **"The Ethics of Artificial Intelligence"** by Boddington Paula
   A detailed examination of the ethical questions surrounding AI development and use.
2. **"Superintelligence: Paths, Dangers, Strategies"** by Nick Bostrom
   A forward-looking perspective on the potential and risks of advanced AI systems.

Articles and Reports

1. **"AI for Humanity: Building Ethical and Responsible AI"**
   Published by the World Economic Forum, this report explores global efforts to ensure ethical AI development.
2. **"The Stakeholder Capitalism Metrics"** by the International Business Council
   A guide to measuring ESG performance for businesses aiming to align with stakeholder capitalism principles.

Online Resources

MOOCs and Courses

- **"Elements of AI" (Free Course)**: A beginner-friendly introduction to AI, offered by the University of Helsinki.

- **"AI for Everyone"** by Andrew Ng on Coursera: A non-technical overview of AI's applications and implications.

Websites

- **Partnership on AI**: A multi-stakeholder initiative dedicated to responsible AI practices.
- **AI Now Institute**: Focused on the social implications of AI technologies.

Research Papers

- **"Algorithmic Accountability"**: Examines frameworks for holding AI systems and their developers accountable.
- **"Ethics Guidelines for Trustworthy AI"** by the European Commission's High-Level Expert Group on AI.

Videos and Podcasts

1. **"AI and the Future of Work" (TED Talk)** by Kevin Roose: Insights on AI's impact on the job market and how businesses can adapt responsibly.
2. **"The AI Alignment Problem"** by Robert Miles: A YouTube channel dedicated to explaining the complexities of aligning AI systems with human values.
3. **"Exponential View" Podcast by Azeem Azhar**: Explores the intersection of technology, business, and society.

By leveraging these resources, leaders and professionals can stay informed about the evolving role of AI in shaping stakeholder-driven business strategies. These appendices collectively provide a roadmap for navigating the opportunities and challenges of AI in a rapidly changing world.

END

www.ingramcontent.com/pod-product-compliance
Lightning Source LLC
Chambersburg PA
CBHW071433220526
45469CB00004B/1512

and as a disruptor that can challenge traditional business models, ethical frameworks, and workforce dynamics.

ISBN 9798302616999

COLTIVAZIONE IDROPONICA

MANUALE FACILE E COMPLETO PER IMPARARE DA ZERO CON LE MIGLIORI TECNICHE AGGIORNATE

Testi Creativi
Scrittura con Passione